Symphony
for Human Transport

Other works by Lisa Samuels include:

LETTERS (Meow Press 1996)
The Seven Voices (O Books 1998)
War Holdings (Pavement Saw Press 2003)
Paradise for Everyone (Shearsman Books 2005)
Increment (a family romance) (Bronze Skull Press 2006)
The Invention of Culture (Shearsman Books 2008)
Throe (Oystercatcher Press 2009)
Tomorrowland (Shearsman Books 2009)
Mama Mortality Corridos (Holloway Press 2010)
Gender City (Shearsman Books 2011)
Wild Dialectics (Shearsman Books 2012)
Tomorrowland CDs (Deep Surface 2012)
Anti M (Chax Press 2013)
Over Hear (TinFish Press 2015)
Tender Girl (Dusie Press 2015)

LISA SAMUELS

Symphony
for Human Transport

Shearsman Books

First published in the United Kingdom in 2017 by
Shearsman Books Ltd
50 Westons Hill Drive
Emersons Green
Bristol
BS16 7DF

Shearsman Books Ltd Registered Office
30–31 St. James Place, Mangotsfield, Bristol BS16 9JB
(this address not for correspondence)

www.shearsman.com

ISBN 978-1-84861-547-2

Cover art by Lisa Samuels: *Atocha Garden*.

Acknowledgements

Some poems in *Symphony for Human Transport* are to be published in
Hambone (ed. Nathaniel Mackey), *Upstairs at Duroc* (ed. Barbara Beck),
and *women: poetry: migration [an anthology]* (ed. Jane Joritz-Nakagawa),
with thanks to the editors.

Contents

One   9

Two   23

Three   43

Four   59

I finally dreamed last night
after waiting years to repeat my life
in copies under dark and light
in the dream there were familiars and machines
one took thinking and assembled it
like tiny death-ray octopi welded to a self
they stretched out in translation for the watchers
in the dark spotlight of the dream
the door of the train flew open

ONE

♮

The door of the train flew open and we walked
  grass and trees without knowing
     wings inside the brain   who flutter out
        all you present for what I hear
       the recognition forcing to an edge?   I cannot hide dislodge
       make room for me   no explanations understand of earth

 we surged out tripping over sky sounds
        mind trees flowers leaves dirt
   the world interpreting itself to each other
   across the tops of buildings flying with our feet
      tressed delicate through we flew
       the green tops of the sky bespoke
the warm day held no countenance for itself
entirely given to burning

♮

The door on the train blew open you stood
silent as the aftershock we came for
in that silent still hit screen pass
   we knew things   we were celebrants fitted at the window
where the smoke and conjuration kept us at it
   kept us to the strings, percussed like the throat on open
lightly thrummed against, a delicate
bashing sound like an announced ascension
parallel an air device diving by the recourse we could make
   were we there   were we at the door
whose munificence has its limit
   were we clear enough, transparent silent
shock crisp in its outlines like the quiet road
terms given as you ask   devices permanent as day

♮

To celebrate the self-devolved concussion
  in that sudden frame
was all the welcome you could want
  to walk in to a question
touch the sideswipe of the rush
    to think   all your body clear as trees
    for that time   clear as what you know
    the spring-held trap sense
in the mind whose color's green and pale
  and blue devouring idea flowered
of its strength   all that duplication
  in the glass the door shines
on the outside where to breathe

♮

The door to the train flew open without semblance

with a rare and sharp-full torso of knowing

myself a blister in the parts, a blister in the parts to move

the door, the spring air blasting its congenital

favor, not a tease, a specified air-fire blast from earth

felt early in the morning tired from the moon

and strung out inside torso's heavy stone

the heavy object moves its sunder slowly

wedged so tight, the blockade of the heart

its night-blind sore the torso an enormous

life's dead conscious-tempered stone

♮

Every hour within the frame of air
the train were monstrance held
to the torso of the groaned idea
             there they went   the bodies walking out of air
      strode within an accident of shaken
         disposition   mouths akimbo
  to the merest question words posed
    on the platform of idea where we stood
             queer as milk   queer as rounded land shapes
       where the train curved fast to loose its prior forms
from any door struck through with flesh
from any window holding light-hit air
               the eye bathes morning through
       the moving sky exceeds the blank

♮

The door of the train moved open
voice chattel with the title full behoove
we listened for weeks the edges in our fold
    we were open   listen to the gentle door
    fixed on electric command

our bodies sere bound where we were
on mantra's perfect scale
       streaming judging clear calm full of noise
the sounds in my head were tree bark growing
faster than the sun shot through
    the door outwhere I flew   hands holding air

soft than light we walked our bodies
  somber tropey knowing it the mouth
  burned slow dislocation's afternoon

♮

The gnomon spoke outside adoring partly open partly
close to air strung taut on the dippled edge
    dependent on the doorish breeze
  infusing inside out   *a gnomon we could really count*
    the train were lexical to nuance
    in that tight saw fully down
 our want   the edge-cut fullest sheet of doors
  were smacking open closed the parts dement
 the water without glass   without pane
     smiling no more clear   transparent, no more clear
like dominance untouching its own walls
the world's already other half tore slow away
  the trees their candid caliber stand quiet
  near the door they know no more

♮

Our own crash on center's law
   you crash   the law of others near us
  wrap more merciful near the train door self
  extrusion clear and stripped from
      doorways   trains   mobs   flutes
struck over and over on the tracks
whose trains played for them smashing
  wings of break strike flashing on the sky
    flat-backed near consequence
  we were true as
               daybreak on the city
  high above the tracks where flutes yield up
  their incremental sounds they're made to make
   and then they quieten   they quieten   surtout
the body flit not breaking toward the thunder
     not more bent curve track
  rushed in the sweet air spring
of thunder through the mind's construe

♮

The door to the train flew open
we walked kindly gentle talking habits
at our ease a young voice without mercy
curls adjacent to the memory
black road curling through the houses
without speed they track   no road
    spoke open language out
    of safety's fullest music crossing   melismatic
    streets walk upright peeling off the ground
    they're laid on sideways thick and full
the branches break the window
staring out   the asphalt's bare alive
our breathing pillowed like an umbrage
darling fire warm and soft as icicles on the brain

♮

The train wide advent and the life
opinioned on the day inside
  hover much transparency
  prise out an unapproach
  meant on the heart

    our spackling hite
    promise light were flick
    height litheness that were
    sleep – the calm wind
    carriage dormant
   frames sheet soft
  as skin a window
  crushing light then glows
 in front of the door
the train blew open

♮

The door on the train flew open over the flowers
carnacs green things and starwhites
spigot turned on all the animals rush out
half-toned beasts excited smile voluminous
bearing up the heart outside the body
gently nail it to the clouds above us
flickering in its pitch – the cloud mouth
wants to eat or drink contusion gape here with
the domes and shake a pitted shift
that holds my mouth the open lungs
they breathe so fine now they are bare
without confining skin or heart
they breathe their habitation near
your flanks outflanked of gold

♮

The door on the train flew open and the world rushed in
  sweet scents obliterating sense's body
   holding leaves trees branches   the road
the perfect time of non-ordinary life

   the door on the train flew open
   spring with its obliterant magnitude instantly around us
      and our hair fell out   we were deployed
    we walked under the incessant magnitude of spring
   in a fixation of destruction   eyes flown from the head
       not given back light   spring invades
      our minds invivid layering inside again
and again the mind at once makes time

TWO

♮

The door to the train blew open and I landed sore on cue
torn to an angle quadrate from the orders

precisely no denominator strode through firing
disestablished life with my directives in it, striding

on this view one ordinarily talks of points, wobbles, lines
cut by punctimonious insistences *like this and this*

not like that, we need to meet the century's
Have Been Might Strode, whose description
warrants resembling not only choral scurries but
everyone tanking the brief assembly for ex-self

the train making no sound in the arrival shock
suspended, the senses disarray their pointers, ride like froth
on screeds writ in the metal of the train
whose car becomes a leitmotif of scratched-out mental stuff

♮

The branches were our arms replaced
inside the sky invisible from the door where eye clouds
see the spring feel near what made them ope

    the sky was friendly with the trees
   in fact within the branches   blue sift in the leaves
       for sky a high sound reach   a hover in its arms
  a sphere of distance having
                      now beside the train
  the svelte cut narrowed   wider for an instant
     cut from stride to know   our ears were perked
     to hear the dovetail of a bird near
pretty for your bliss-align bud   flowers tight on know

    amassing from the thick cull cut of bodified air
      the parsec spring   I mean that door
of which our own ideas train on open chance

♮

The train flew open *ting*

   the tink thing flinched

   and scored long strings

drawn on a think curve

  plink what you utmost   move

    put your fingers there and draw

      the note toward you, pull it

with the long bow   here do your most

      stage and arrival up

    and mid-sound round

      stacked to the mouth's electric

   ring you stand door open

     joy's toy sonic   leaves rush in

     a long sound for this   hear

♮

The crack's embedded moment makes a parabole
　on tracks whose train was feeling
　　　to be with, to be welded　with a hurry for the flash time
　　　it was spark with gas explosion
　　　refted to the tracks the cracks showed sky
the train was going stolid　brass　upstart we stood
beneath the door glass breaking place

　　　the spring day's sky face turned outside
　　its new assumption bells accreting cost or hours
　　　folded in devotion's onspell　near us　　too near
　　　　meant a sign were　　*we had moved near its combined authority*
　　depending how it looks we might re-curl
　　　near the sober woman's tread
　　　a mirror　codes for benediction

♮

The door to the train flew open day
            threw its disk into   the air
        caught and sent it to the clouds
            absorbing gently they said
come and see idea and I knew them   I was for it

the grasses rise bearing the dispersed clouds
    (inside them we walk tinier than the eye
behind the holding air little green things
crush a path through the back of the world

        click clack   (making tracks the side on disappear
the side were ornaments pollen bags
dirt spheres wagging tree leaves
    from devotion's tide   the crusts of grasses
        scattered waves of earth

♮

The ears flew open
listening for the whoosh
half-apparition people there
subtiding you stood
streaming in imagined air
hands held up streaming
near the train of spring
low mountains covered with fur
amidst whose delicate haunts
we could sub-line partaking
in the air we flew the door
around us shaking in its instruments
abandoned fleet shook to the tracks
the strings around my torso held
and lifted up that shot
the brain the open
thought-door's *whoosh*

♮

The mental atmosphere streams
      out from micro-done
           to polymaths of love
whose hands warm plants reach
        plunked within the ground
            that not forgets itself
the plants are red
      pink pondering
         blur green grey
brown broad fit
    sharp   husked fair

      the plants are spinning they collapse
lovely they are shoots with pardon
      floated up
        re-stoved inside the body's
gentle supertone forever
      only it's never not different
        always the tone rises   new plants
uniform
    bubbles in blown rooms

the heads move closely
      where the plant-rooms
        gorgeous earphones fit
the train cars long and
    clipped the frame door
      where the body's split

in multiple
        tree stumps large by sky
                whose soft leaves fracture trees
  where birds fly magnets
      where their wings
           huff where the tight sounds
of their wings huff in
      the magnet air
           where breath's too fast for birds

♮

The train flew open hand in hand stark of water
standing there were strew perts   naming uplands
opening as they can the frame keeps wand-flipped
  strewn as
                 we are capable of   imagine restive sensate glare
                 part-time as obstacles yet so solid
  off-screen by the breach not heated
    by the spring door not at all

  your head turned to the air rush
          train flown open without sound
the body narrow on the seat
perched without any trope
one could not see   the country curled in itself
        taught sense   *I mean what happens in the fit*
      cut air-stream incorruptible   all through us
         recognition   daze of centuries
     offering books to tell the time

as though clarity opens   face by face
planetary timing strapped impatient
to the rivets of the train   without more rush
     with everyone's nonobvious
       pelts clept shaking in the meaning   meaning

you open your ears there's always sounds
the additive wail of sound   we hear in
     beached astride doing all we can to render

tearable   our brains open to look that urge
turns into   words turn out
to trill your ears with having
known   the curtains shortly rush
the still air wall of green that wants toward you

♮

The door to the train flew open seemly state
found us by the skin
    true to be slighted   aslant on time
  regents of flowers gave truce
     and twice-supped proof made flesh
      to grow there   sip sup
   now you're bee-kept
   you got the honey-greens
   graft in air slice *hup*
       ungathered to conduct   the train
flew where the bellows place
by accident   I mean they're stuck most serious
    I mean the ground's amirror
  soft earth crumbles in its lease

♮

The train's flown head rolled off into the blue
trance greenly lit itself   a greeny fire
       (you catch that near enough the strew
          spring caps when you outname it   (that's the kind of

flat-out head-fly up it went, the head so pert
       it held the sky green tracks in line
so everyone would be fed
                          the leaves sparked inside
(like the child cries and thus creates a world
          shift pips to rule out danger
          make the sources do the big reveal

that's the train I found myself in
    the recessive voice trancing
       to a whirl that knew how to answer
  how to sing   make a ticket   buy something soft
throw the leaves into the corner of the room, do that

       finite train whose apparition felt
       the self-strewn dogma of softest possible
          daylight air   turn scents
       beyond illumination's power to explain
                the daw hands flicked for mass polarity
       daw hands possible atop
                the stony tower (so much later still

much later still the soft
heart's hard tremble stuck on fit
it's stuck   the lunar subdivisions split
          the head's ordeal too strafed
     for one's attention to   fit clear
     the trembling of that outer mind
               a brain on anyone's rim trope
(you can see it hear it   you can totally relate this
   very near your own full
thick mind's body   disappears beneath
itself the cloths wrapped round as though
there's nothing   underneath it   anyway
     that's the train's adore
   the frame door out the train
through which I flew

♮

The door to the train flew open and the light broke

    your face splintered as it was

  on making croft shanks

   flit with full consumption

the croft shanks lit themselves in flashes

never more produced the wet thread

    crested art's florescent

     more than felt   a crescent door

   the arms held out   the body held that pose

transparent   lucid accident the trees

     replaced your body and were height

   strings   strained a little tensed

    in a pain ground   not sure to plant their sensitives

  for the wind to toss in many leaves

to gift themsevers   instrumental

coping on the building of the hill

whose holding drag's fair   tenuous   all grown up

the dirt-flesh growling underground   all copers

like the dirt-brain   push through searched-out

microfields   inside their clasp

air cages gentle bodies   doing hath broke

spun croon   shonking in the city

grievous beauty we'd come to stand

your life quiescent purpose   giant by   compare

whole catchments turn spruce   through the breaks

a large sound sculpture   ready for   as anything

♮

The door to the train flew open and the sweetest possible
scent furled in

           then I was in a garden and the parlor-game
split open that scene

            then we were piloted, the pilot game
fiery and unveiled us we were furled we skanked it
held our mouths closed with personal kite loft

what we were to do was close our mouths
with our hands we held our tongues
with our fingers and the animals stared wondering
what scents merge with the cloud-stream
whether talkative in that other possible
                    plum change whether
living force could tolerate ourselves shanked in

the door totally smiling without eyes it smiles technological
to accept its surety for were we there
             we played that
obsolescent stream provide a play-list we could check
against a glee before-scorched-path ourselves float out?

so spleen turns fit the scheme path with soft sides
we were touching base

                    touched inner, the blind animal
scent whose outer trees burnt version
magnetize the disarray the body diamonds in

that blind tent in the cool reverse
day piloting I felt almost along the side of earth
whose planetary dreaming turned the whole
alight, a techno flight sound roars
at night's strange city
    honks and bloats of night
machinery proves the loud void
tactics juice the disarray the body
gilds far in

♮

The door to the train blew open and the sun shone
intently in the obscured fire of its original
undoing, we saw the fire build
standing in the thick window
where earlier creatures stared for us
the sun were staring through them
to the door – there it was and then again silence
through breath assent and antique life
the far-off cliffs walk through the sun
the soft pads met each other absolutely alive
in that time, soft crystalline flesh doing-undoing
an invert of the lateral door whose cope held trees
inside its form deep consonants
pressed together by the face

THREE

♮

The door to the train flew ope and I bedecked
bedoomed in the embrasure klept or kind
small creatures given to semble
gave themselves agaunt to semble
crew merchants gathering up tight animals
to gleam, or so I toughed

I thoughed in the clear wreck of day
lathed on the quell, organic as instruments
never against never agon sway
the stars looking very much like planets
lick the back side of the galaxy
with enormous tongues made of planets
making fumy holes the planets milling gorging
out of the way of the tongue suck
swills the energy of naught

the door for the trained half flew
half smiled in arches flicked
mind plenty for its dull pinch
ready for the match table call
haps make the cards flow down the sound
of flicky haps togetherer

the doors held sharp as rain
wet on the cross hatch fleck modes
dawdling by day, quiescent as the moon chains
hitting out night's fire wraiths

turning all those leaves to ash
where ash betides its pearly outlines
truly through

♮

The train flew outward   we could hear
the door wings flint the sky   scrape on
          the sides   surround a new harmonic
     cloud arms   cast a surface premise up
a fragile cache inside the door
          a vocal thick assemble   *it's a kind of people*
     expressive   *enter in the widest voice*
               we heard her language doublement
smoothly at the door the wait
          a thousand ear pitch we decline
trackside builders   ringing in the world

♮

The door flew open the exceeding air
    cedes   bifurcate assembly   touches
pads on firmament equal to   pleas
    perorate   mantras gather around the trees
       put clothing on and off and on
  too on the far note   language stranged
   position in a separate spring   her text
accentual travel aggregate   in the chant
attention's micro-scopic scent desports
    enthusiastic on the vocal
      echoes up and down   the world's return
  recession breathable metallic
getting-somewhere things don't make to hoard

♮

The door of the train blew open repeat
ach in the spotlight of the given dream
like opening a bag to see   explode
    the bag's content hovers glows
its angel dark by spring

as on blue the glow's determinant
keeps you provender
releasing notes for   placate
    shunts swift copy
from the mammals of the place

they're doggish they inhabit
mind's unlanguage like
a copy given out to wet enormity
    that's what the animal knows
    embracing the adventured trees
their honey-pads up high
and out of sight because historical

they give you quiet topical guard
delayed experience
humming positives below

♮

The door to the train without
plans in that direction becomes
portal to a posture banded white-
sheet-tight in a non-absorptive matter
of tremendous flex that then reconstitutes
what seems important to do next – for that
the band becomes a crux of wherewithal defining
neither back nor forward but a spread of being with-
out interruption's continuity and yet
and yet the person

♮

The stance the person totally inhabits

every part of time's bent palette's dense increase

whose vincible solitude chimes itself

    a gentle part direction rose

so that a person played by landscape

stands for bodies at the train

where harbingers known as micro-portent

    set on sky flit back

the short machinery of the ears

re-eye the sky where bodies tumble

anchored to their mirrors

    rose-air rises in the outside

    blank skirt trees they rise

♮

The train flew open

smiles turned resonant machine

the unplugged ludic tune (swerved

people-ward the instrument were thoughtful

had a wish to loft the bodies up

an implicate suspension that's the very nature

live, reaching back with my warm hand

turned to film, it reaches through

with smiles touching para-theater flesh

warm blood's pulse on the soft seat

hovering bodies howsome (numerous near each

♮

The door on the train flew   other words
obeyed the transparent gleam of yes
gave its sugar to the natural numbers
    tore fair life from its fat seat
grooming   grooming totally deep-held leaves
the fabric of nearby trees
believing their fair build can hear
    electric wind drunk through the sun
given to their tonals via waves
that rivet air for us to hanker by
    both being and making that fell track
we store our bodies willing to the box
of transport   clack and open shred

♮

The minute crashes fractured
sound waves bluntly through
the glass in tiny tremulate
so true to the vibrations
of the motion twirling
twirling as against the vibrant
leaves the light hit in and
through up down on grasses
tucked so quiet floor
the world do pamper clust
the grasses close *you see them*
hardly intimate in the small ray
look cut from your eye
rays fast in that short moment
barely time to clock
so ope so shh the hove

♮

The door is clear blue hanging there
with nothing to impart but aperture
      blew off its hinge electric   sky mind
   speaking in electric be   to bridge that be

the train blew open without smiling
clear blue struck its chord
    shut part-way cracked the light
swells looking everywhere   we've heard our eyes
      cleared from confusion to confusion
    in the solitary privilege of the possessed

   as though bodies in the grimace of a yield
outside a chance to see or touch
     the chance to see or touch implodes
the shut mouth targets how to speak

♮

To ascribe the inner workings of the glass
stuck to your eye   you pull and pull
it's going here serene attached
  the strew part's keen absorb picks up
your relevant car descried for seconds
  hefted out toward macro-time
  the train again made door's sublime
material density   so then it's true, it's true
the held-tight eyes of daylight
speak dull gold   fine animals wash through
  with a warm bag of small terror
as we fleece for sheeted blue-tides
where the small bags gather kin to arms
    kin to blue-tide declarations
  hovering in the mind's relay
  to starwash magnitudes
so that the car frame black and shiny
with the mystified expression on its front
is life's self-reverence really
  swaying from the page

♮

I breathed inside a wall of green
the door bestrewed   the one road head
quite quarried we renewed ourselves terrain
it was so pretty   sane and tethered to the universe
we sailed like baby weeks
we punched the air's agreement train
cars way up high
we felt near them   ourselves
an angular   sound infused on sense
to hover all coeval
liking angular meeting   inexactly
violet in our doings without wreak
the time not time nor we together weaving seamed

♮

The door on the train blew open and the sky collapsed
from narrow confines gone for breach
that wrangles law from its own self to joy. Come
see the law break open in the sky, the sky's going
breaches out the trees part themselves to see
the doors do open they stay open they detach
themselves like silver from its husk
the golden chapels of the sun lift off
from trees beneath who having waited
now they're wrapped round pure enameling.
It's true I saw it there now trees shake
lifting off that same idea's gold retrace
here they asleep for centuries feel
the ache of traction's joy

FOUR

♮

The door to the train flew open consonance (continents
      on whom the marks of powerful ground
           stood a grave unsmiling face
announce soft paling held in cull

the code spoke heaps, a vibrant flip
            (such pants shirk harmony's fast
      throat to a mode of genuflection
I strip my breathing out to learn

     collaboration's city chance
        chisels a brick on celebrate
(some time to breath to demolition's object
           angle points from fibrous rain
    crossing town in singing bodies
fount unlike what's hearable

♮

The train's grown larger in its depth
an argument like material rose
    paper lifted off the stem   it retrogrades
mass practice   favor   bodies both
      unpresent and re-bloomed
your own mind   as though words were   painted
   scathed arrangement fully live
like wall art typed out   physical
     movement re-spread   *in a certain state*
        the poem most needs to be unwrit
     the open   stet
     on me herein make time
       its score-breaks   repo
    podal call-in where we learn
   retort lights up the trunk
   the phlox unfolds inside
      my hand   the lips speak glove
       turn phrase selected from a heft
  inside a perfect hole where
    meaning lies   outlines
      the same again

♮

The door of the train flew open and the birds call
  sightless without sound the train flock grew
to windows havershaft the many tropes
  clear clasp unmeetable repairs
met in the glass they turn wing
  just in time to make the train blow mix
to skyplots where the acres tend
  fleet elements their friends without more proof
the lightstream flicks more quickly where
  thought's water met it truly choral
the atopical monde implies
  experience tangled with elision's
source-struck subject singing
  capture with the hands

♮

To see by covering dark
and brace astronomy's only gift to us
poor sighted boxwrecks
on our land's intensity
we numerate by kin and doff
by standing on the edge
a mauve intent
a mauve edge marvelous to view
out with the eyes
mistaken from their cramp
in parapets in droves
the blighters' beauties
ravenous to skill to anyone
belfried by a solid stream
the mauve intent's uncovering
things in nature lavish
whether-where the limbs and wings
dive out their chances
strictly for the dark

♮

The tiny ground it opened
 to a scene most like   one's ever clued
  pressed in the sound were gathering   birds
seeking maybe attachment's immanent critique of seeking
   providence   to the ground-spikes   were they?

The door blew open   air-like piking blustery   faces
curious on a consequence   across an entire scale
  given instruments of circles   of organic fable
     many-weathered sweet outer yards
      opening a foreground set out
          darling soi disant humanity
symboled in that flute   aggregate hollow
  succeeding breath   blowing
blows exceeded from a rest

♮

The train in its beatitude
inside its body looking outside air
    elastic full of spring
so full of light the step on life's complexity
to scatter roadways daily flower
                        mirrors constant
doored the train flew (body
gleaming breathing smiling
gorse humanity cranked out

a company – vastation souls girt to our animal's
ship dogmatic that it's cruising
hungry for the main resistance unity might subtide
                        sole blossoms
tread their fury gently near the egress
walk the dew-grey stone shift
blanks whose mirror breathes
the under leaves outside (the train

♮

The door to the train flew open and from far
away the window strained my watch
   a fury of vehicles tiny and catching
    red   grey   white on the smoky barriers
sight whose onyx penetrants could hove eyeballs
were I let them   were I full-tide giant on the window
     over at the far off strokes of action
     in my locks out for out

the cold flames tether each station
out of which   inside which sharp flat
     doubling withstands a blank smile
    in my split skin   tiding there the tiny glass
 and measure edges crystalled on their
doorwaves far aslant

♮

The train flew open thought
neutrinos flank immediate
            they're not mined in lung's conversion
      shot-like in the universe of spent objects
        calling full ideas in the vapor tamp
                  on tamping in a hold

  I mean to say or affirmation's   not-kind ration
      morsel tangled in the mouth whose present push
  to know without control
  the message waiting sur-unbinding   lassoes roped for tethers
        letting go and go   they let our planetary biding
      touch-transmute   each note whose train-flute
      gently rocks the track not moving yet
                  moving all the same, touch hungry
              as we are that castle greenery
            feeds could feel

♮

The door to the train flew out inside the city
scooped it up delicious caliber join-worthy
like the door were fixed atop a high apartment
the city had an answer to that clustering
brake-sounds to the train-sites full of glass
for seeing through ourselves a known
break flat on heaven's hot domain

scooped up we were born there quivering
mense-like brain on electric heat
a kettle or absorptive surface deep
as arrows quiver on their own
deep strew they're targeting
the city par-stroked with a definite
quality of haste, grinding what the given tastes like

the door of the train blew open in a slow
motion braking of the set whose populace
were nicely clearance temporal well
and borrowed languages I start out perfectly rich
my body-money fell out through the holes
that made comparatives temperamental at the least
the air a sign I'd emptied out

♮

The door of the train flew open
site's advancement to align
ourselves effects of noiselessness that sound
so screeching loud in textual ears
we saw it scraping through allowance
ready, ready for the move from car to car
we saw it temporally vincible
dimension darks and lights
exceeded even green broke-open trees
whose light released itself to sky
struck recognition's able stop

the door to the train opened gently
like our ears to entry's ordinary life
come on the ticket takers
recognize you perfect
a contusion of the atmosphere
arrived at retrospective in advance
the car becomes what's clear
for definition's angel ballast here

The door of the train flew open *what*
        we're talking of   we're of a passable talk
of skies hourage vincible   of the person taking count
along the visible   you talk to understand
    contain to our devourment in place
      in harvest's very score   out of your head the world
        cut up and cauterized
                    without a wound, unbalanced
        for a day by day thick firmament
the clay-like screen you carve in tracing
deep-face cuts whose contrast breaks together
        pitch as all afield
        aboard a mute sound
        radius stands

♮

The door to the train flew open measured
far skill flanked to grooming fit
beside our chained-face blind
a smooth flat surface where we count
immeasurement's safe harbor

cut cut, cut cut   cut   it made a sound
intangible to any borrowed waves of air
we walked through with our legs turned into
soughparts, the soughparts were a background
to the retrocussive much where we were wary
and available at once completely knowing
we could not know experience
whose sound was to the pulse we walked
each other's oxygen transformed
a layer much like knowing's letting go

♮

The door to the train flew gently
absence turned to words
ungathering sublate's call beside
a curled tongue the birth
of present's mirror tusk

given to pre-existence karma drags on the known
the pad-like wavy doors
hitting open close, on and off
very near the hands one might exuberate
without closely conching
too near buried earth who knows

the door of the train flew open a thousand doors
left my mind to open into
one by one they opened
thereby no-one else
the trees burn cool, invisible in pantomime
doors retrofit a purpose we could climb into
the record's metaphor unsaid
beside the train whose open door
bejawed exuberate hinge

the animal of life's forgetting
proffered luck
obeisance flaunt
the animal could laugh and call out

words enwrapped with sound's cut honk
the bird strings plucked inside the door
whose train invents its passengers

♮

The door of the train flew open and my mind
quell fires brewing day the mind clean as dirt
beautiful as the soft hair-curled bone
morning opening prinks the naught
night betide the agon still the quietude
inside your mind the life you live come
up to me in song: the day is daylight
in its turn, a plangent fire burn on the skin
a doubled sever counting doubled clouds
beside the hour that dreamed within a dream
house on a cliff, a rental troth bestride the dream
I went within another house also not mine
and sought the earlier dream's high room
the owner time already knew

www.ingramcontent.com/pod-product-compliance
Lightning Source LLC
Chambersburg PA
CBHW031933080426
42734CB00007B/673

9 781848 615472